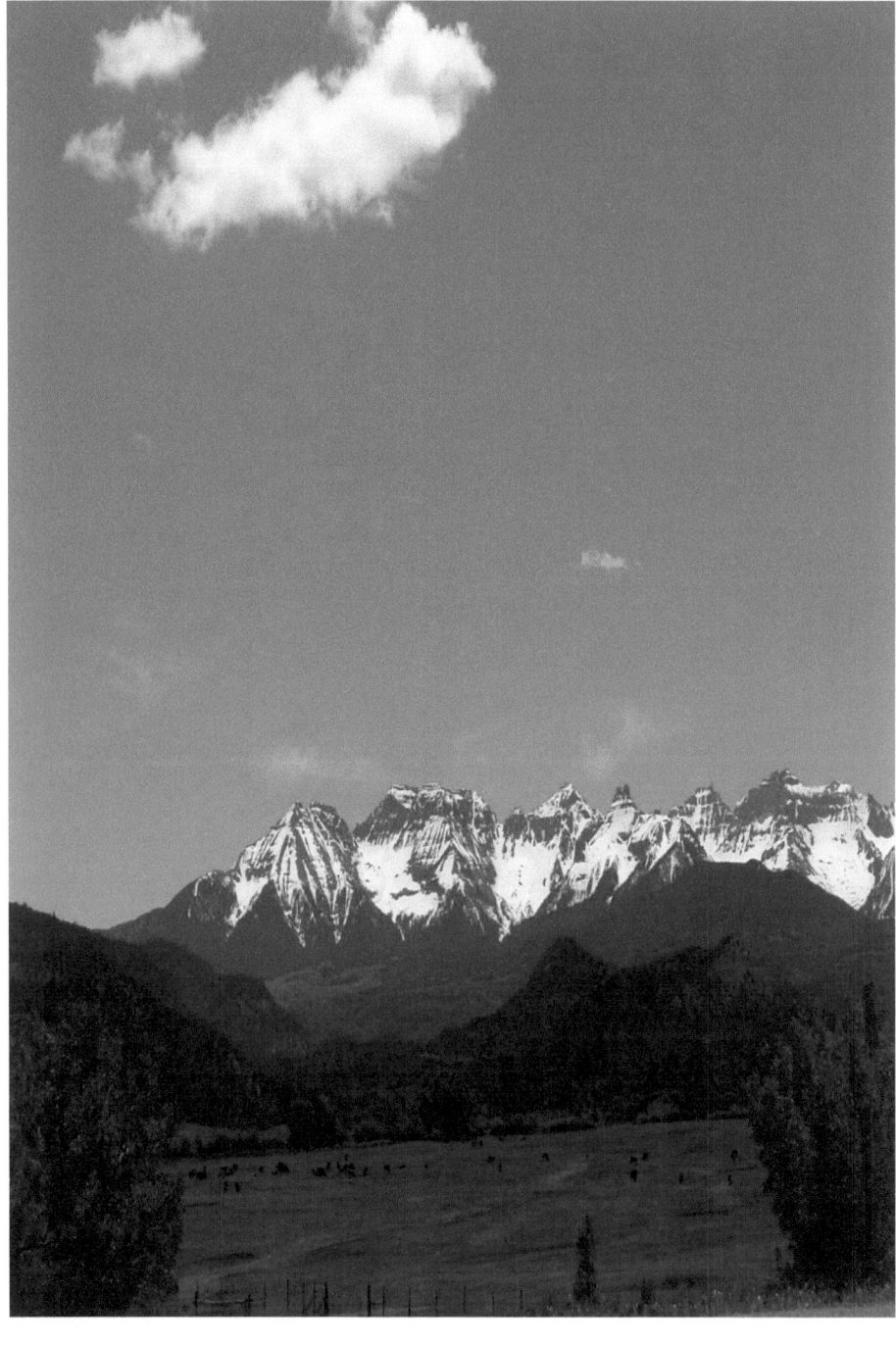

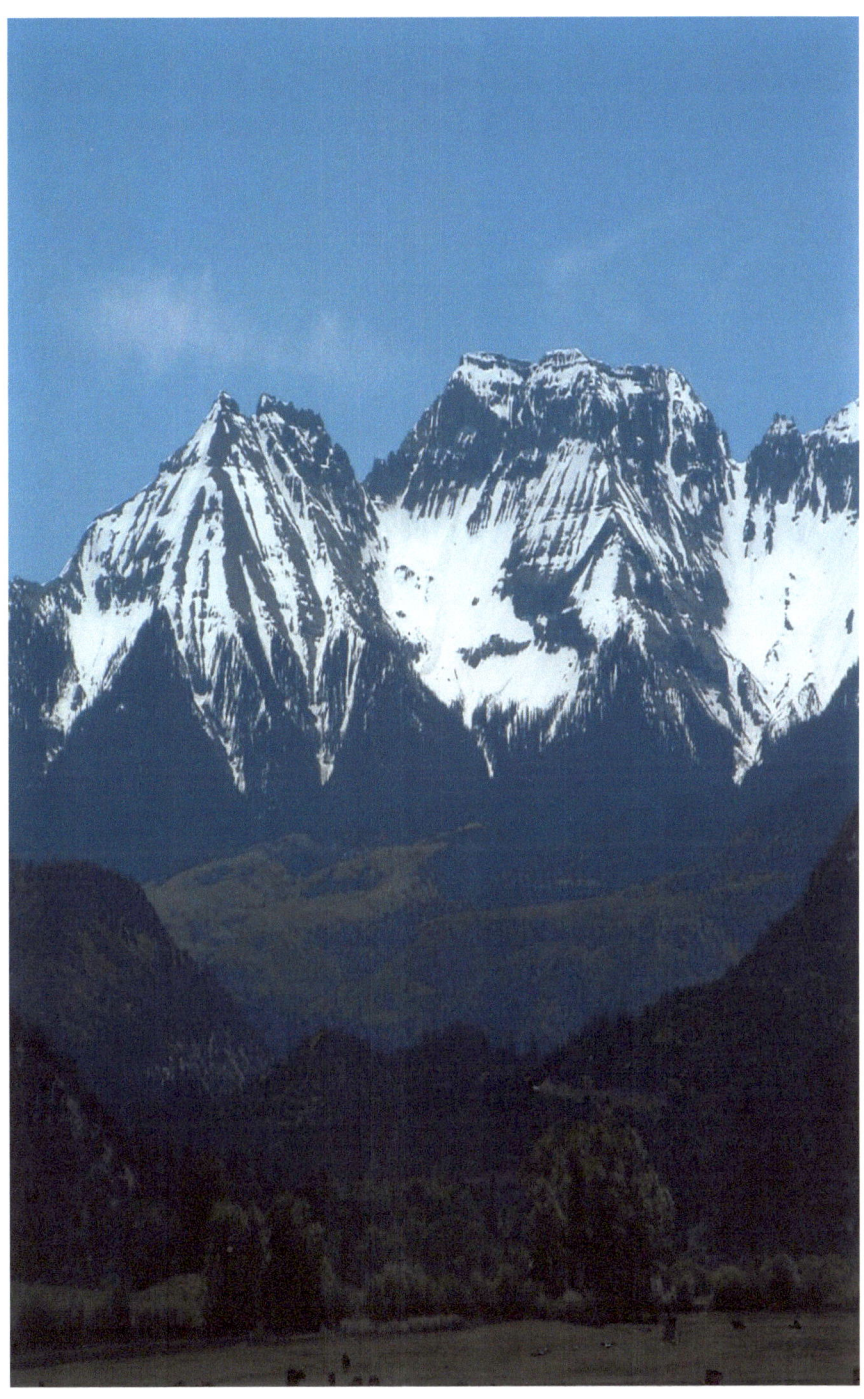

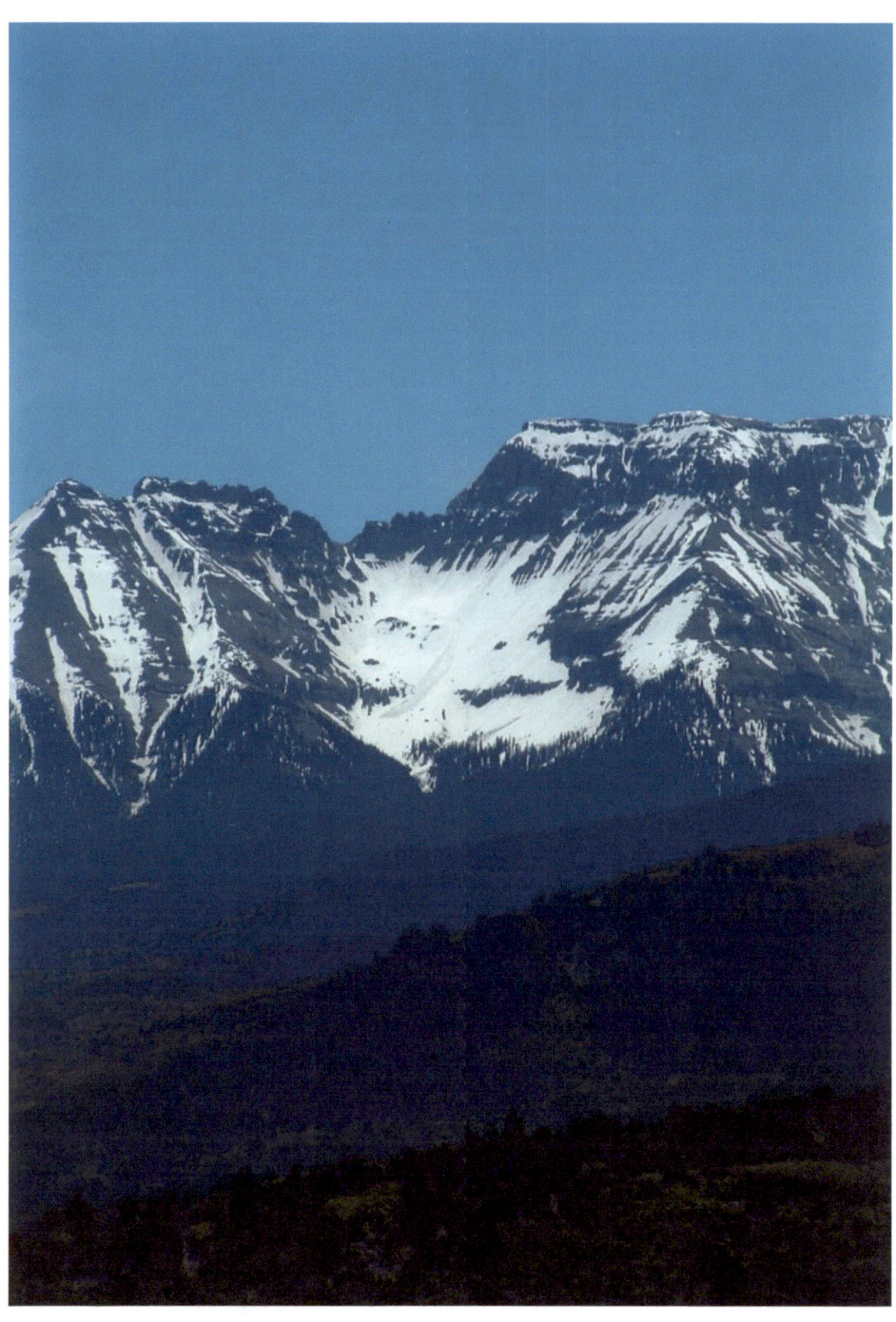

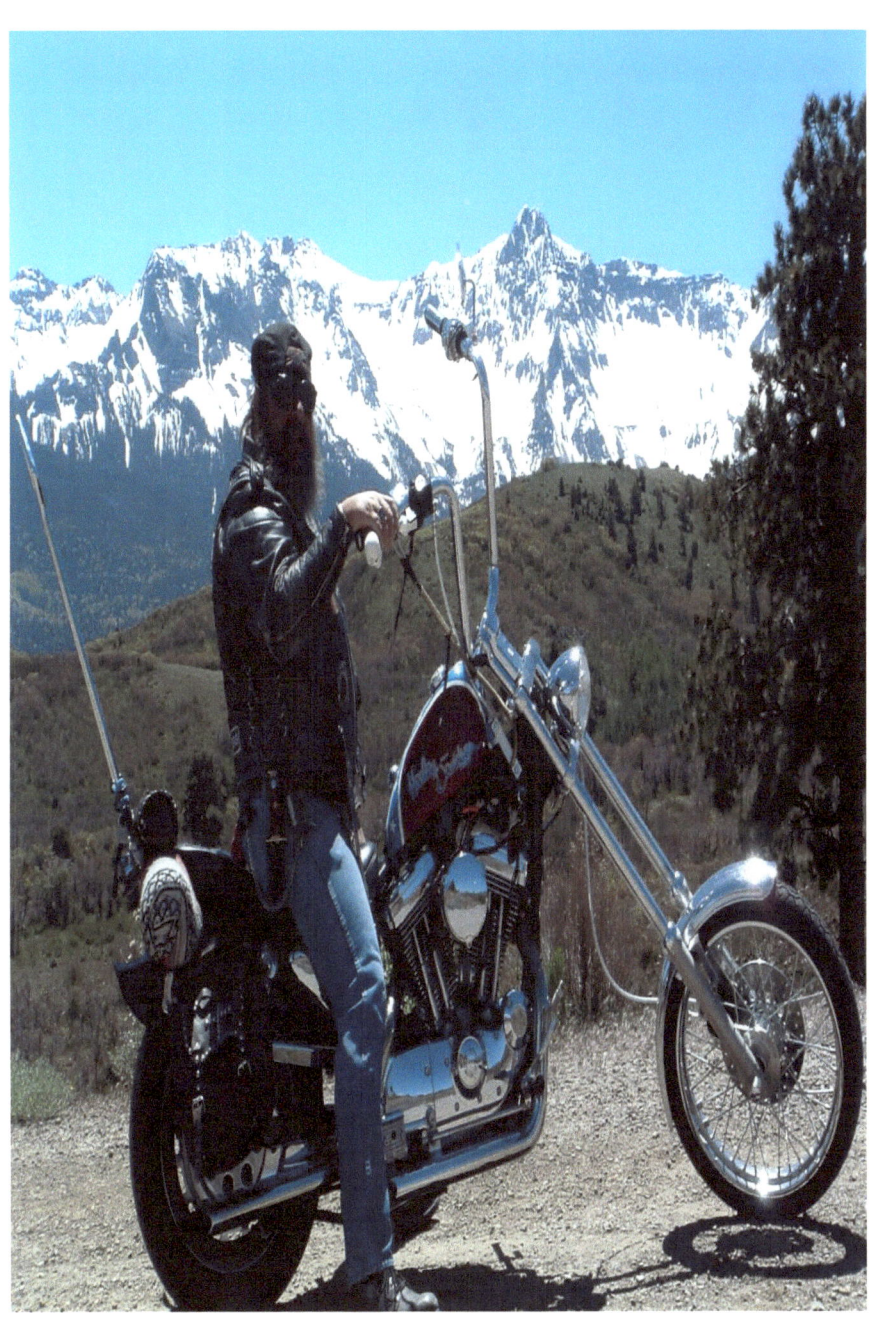

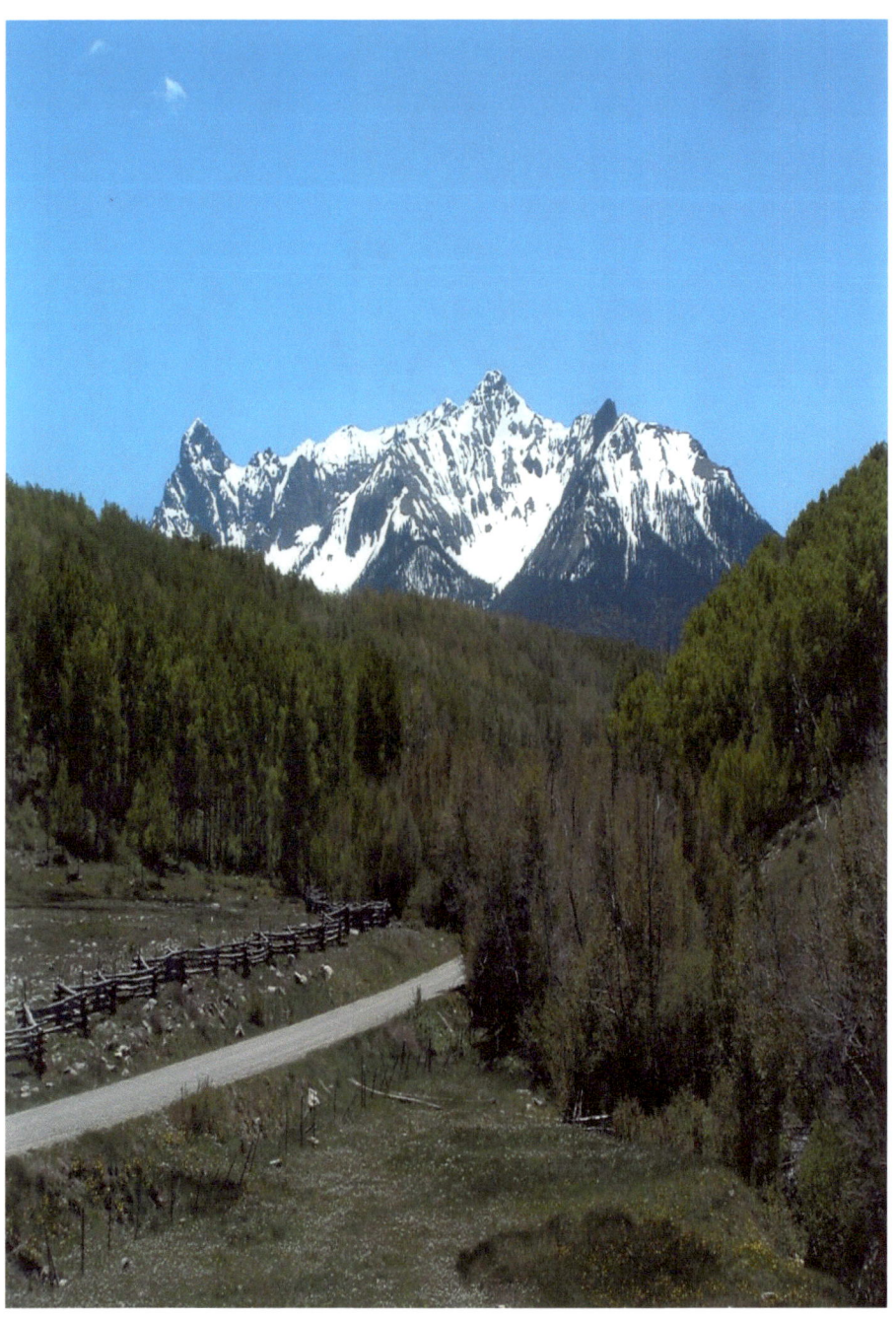

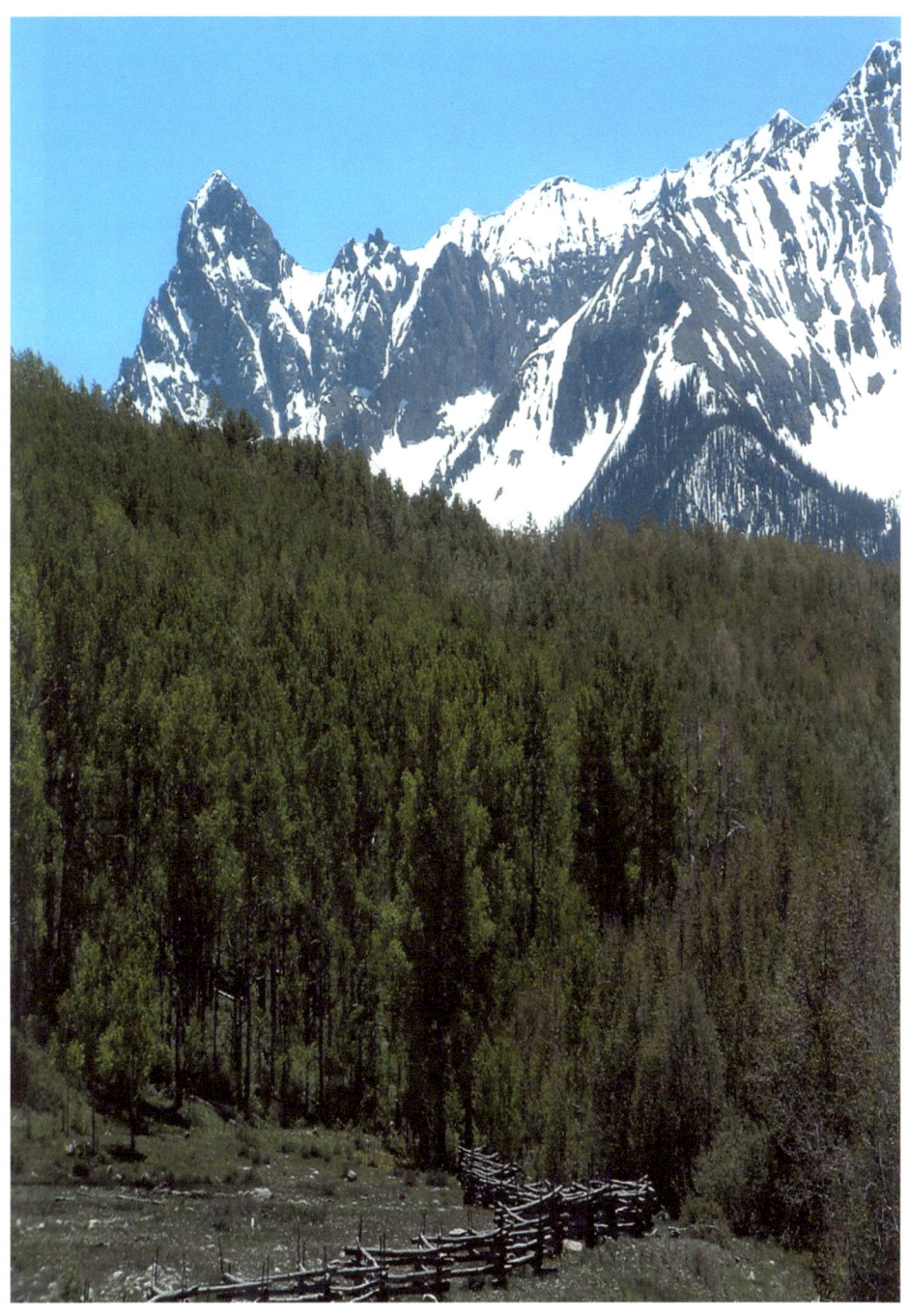

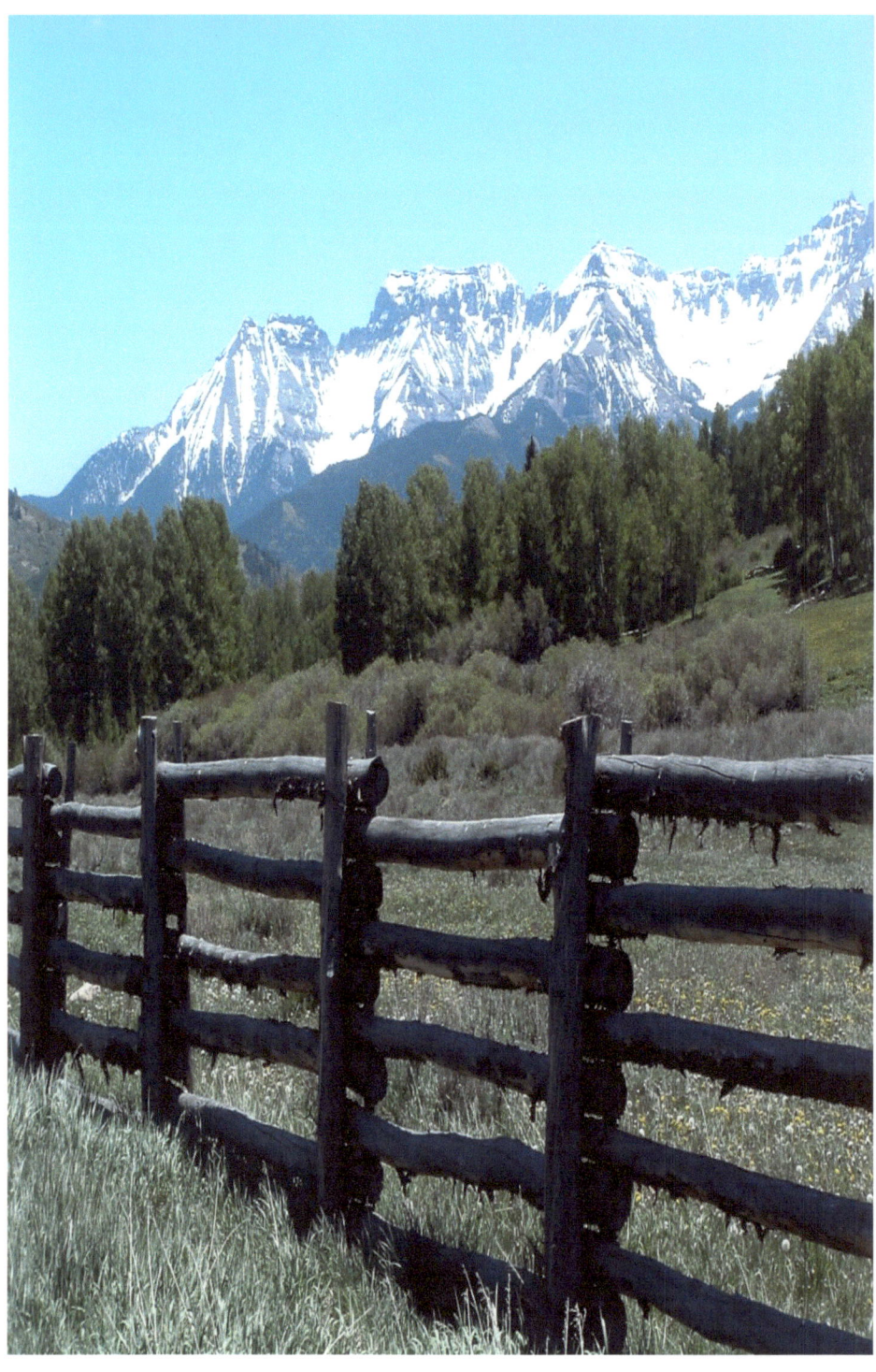

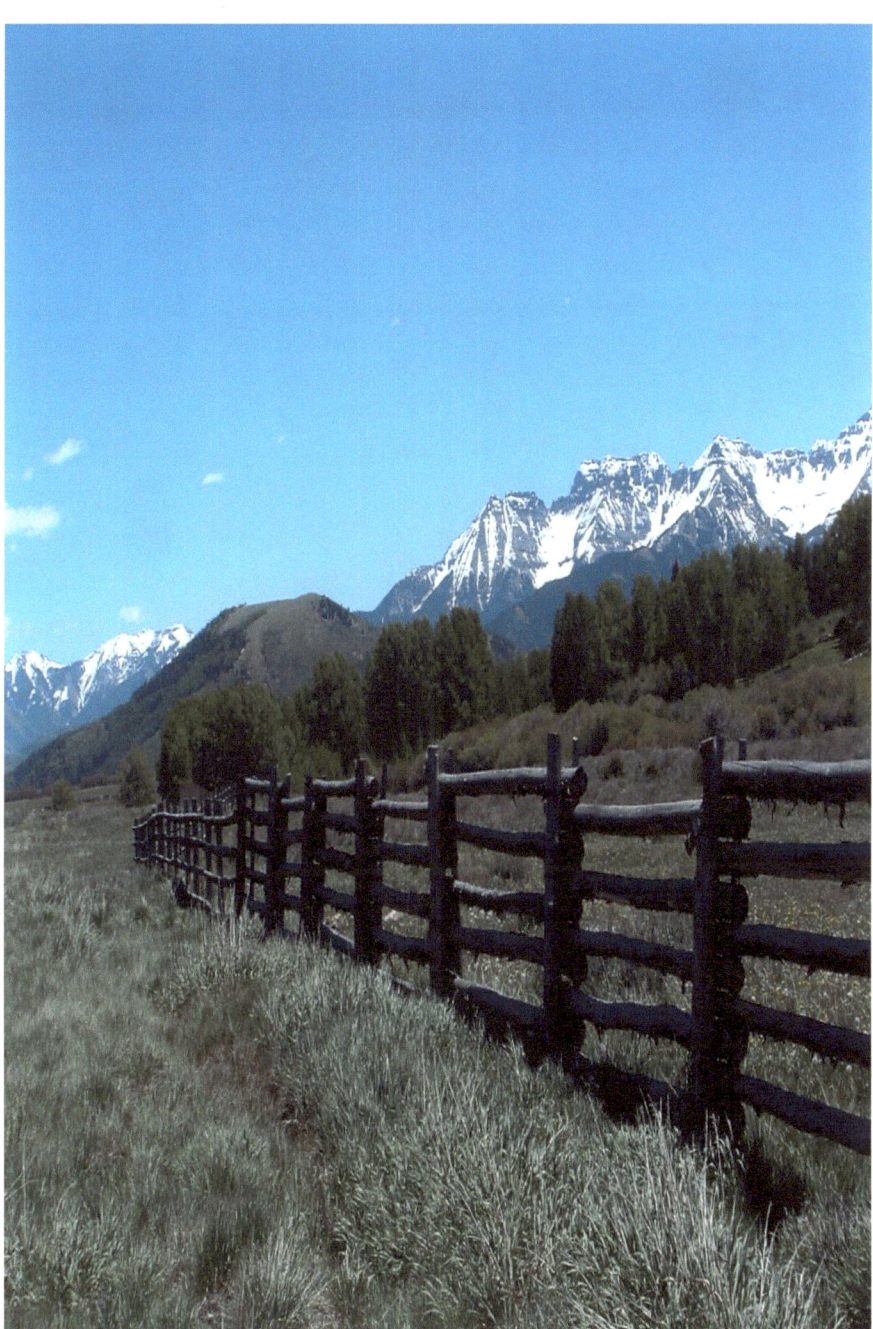

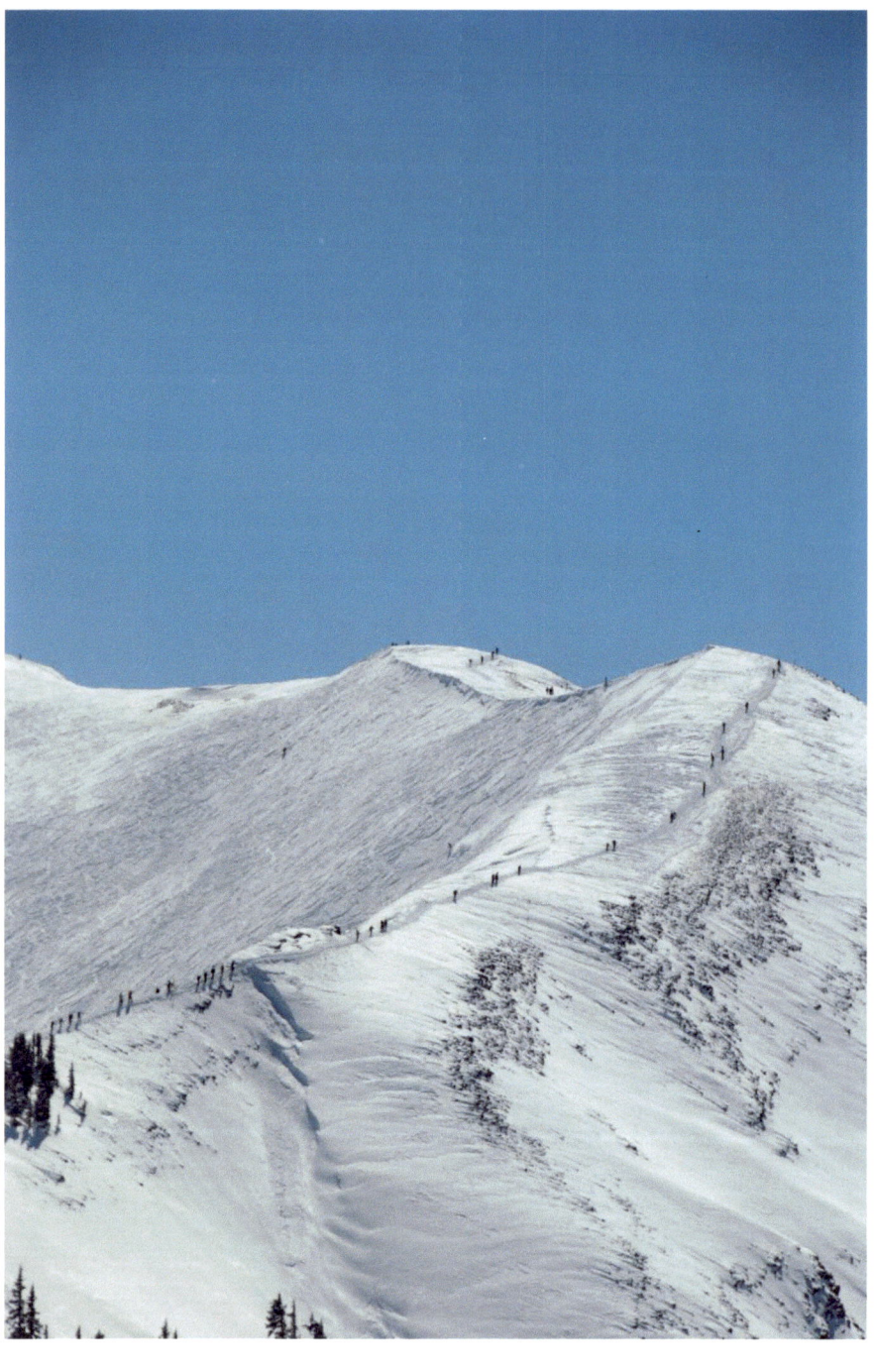

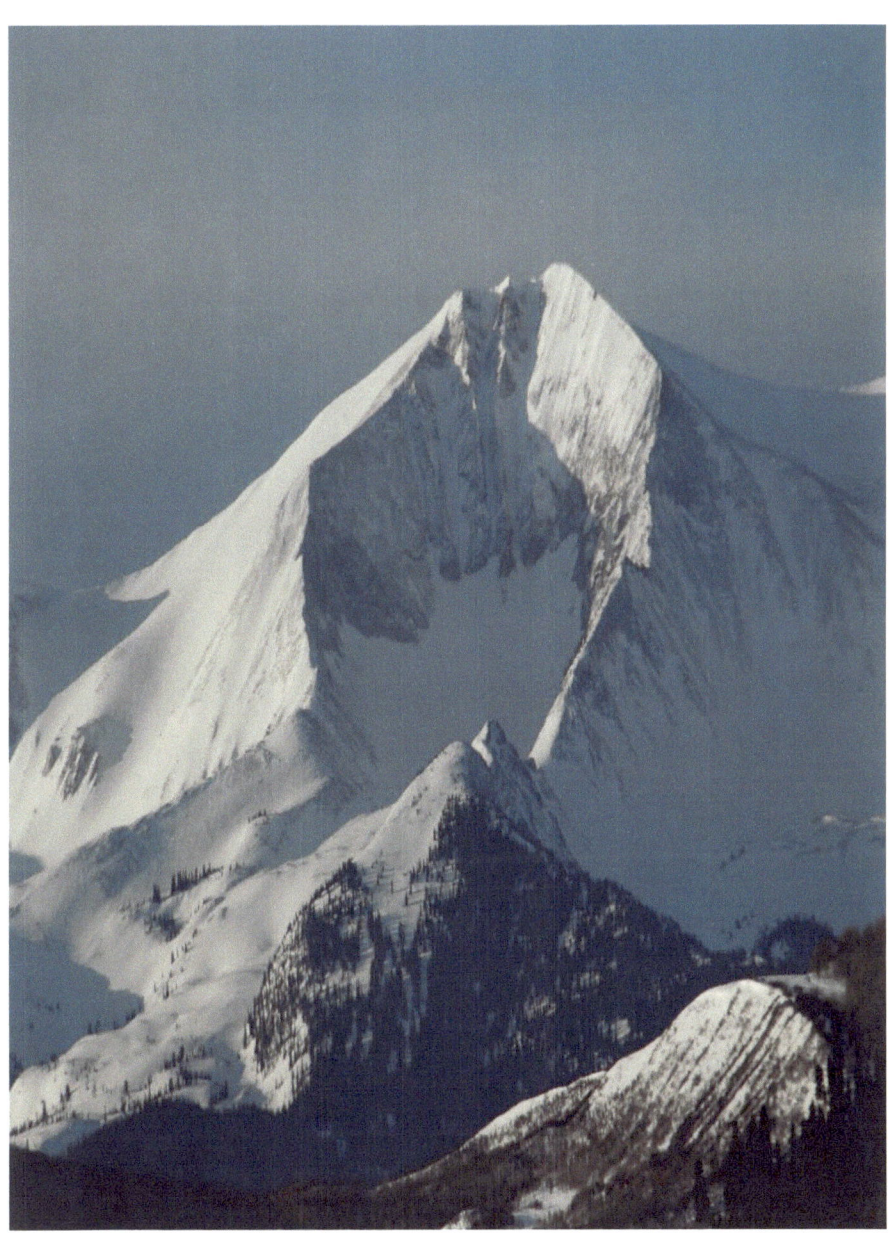

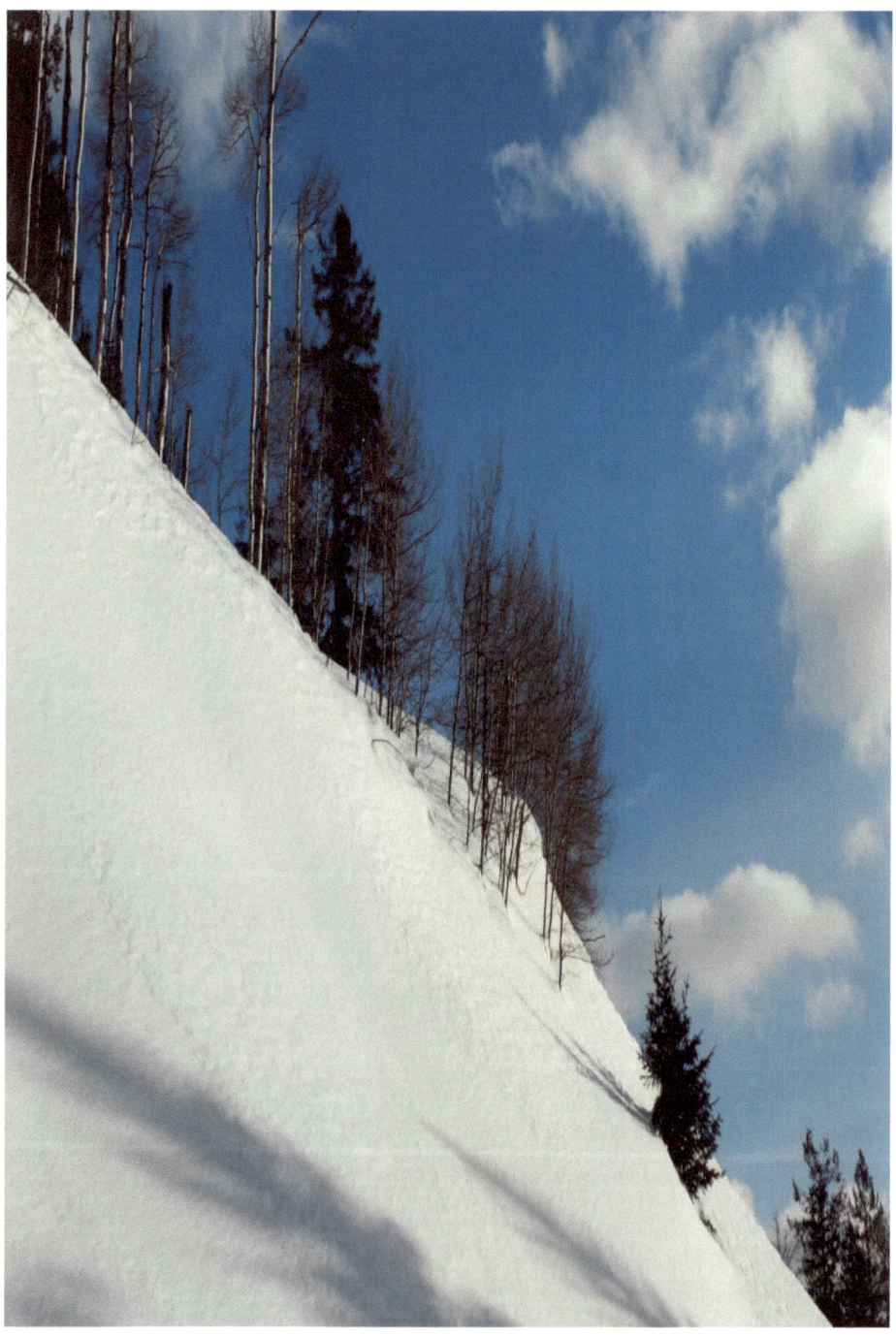

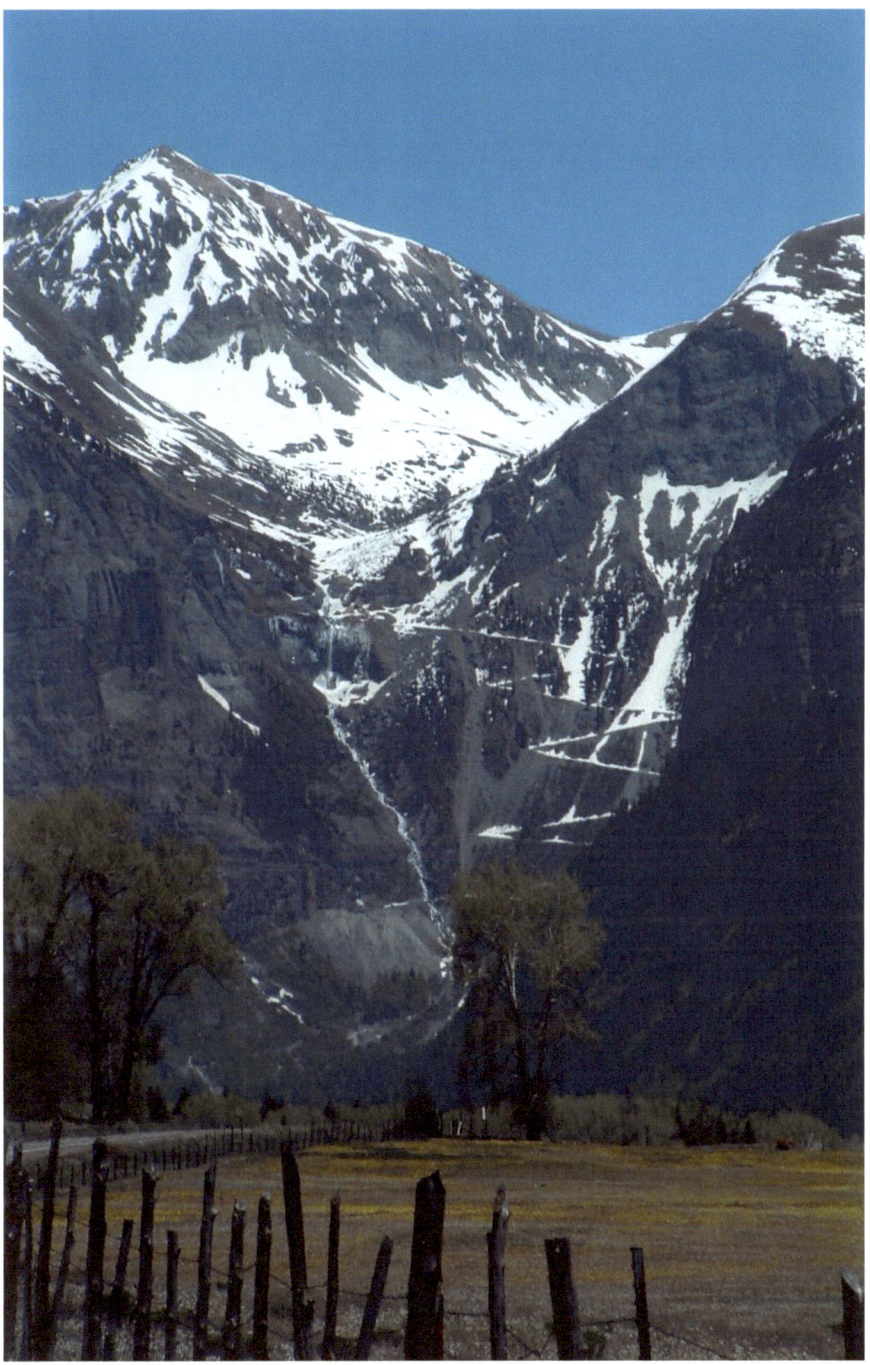

Two ways in and out of Telluride, if you drive, I recommend the way you probably drove in. This in front of you is hells gate pass. I do believe they named it this for a reason.

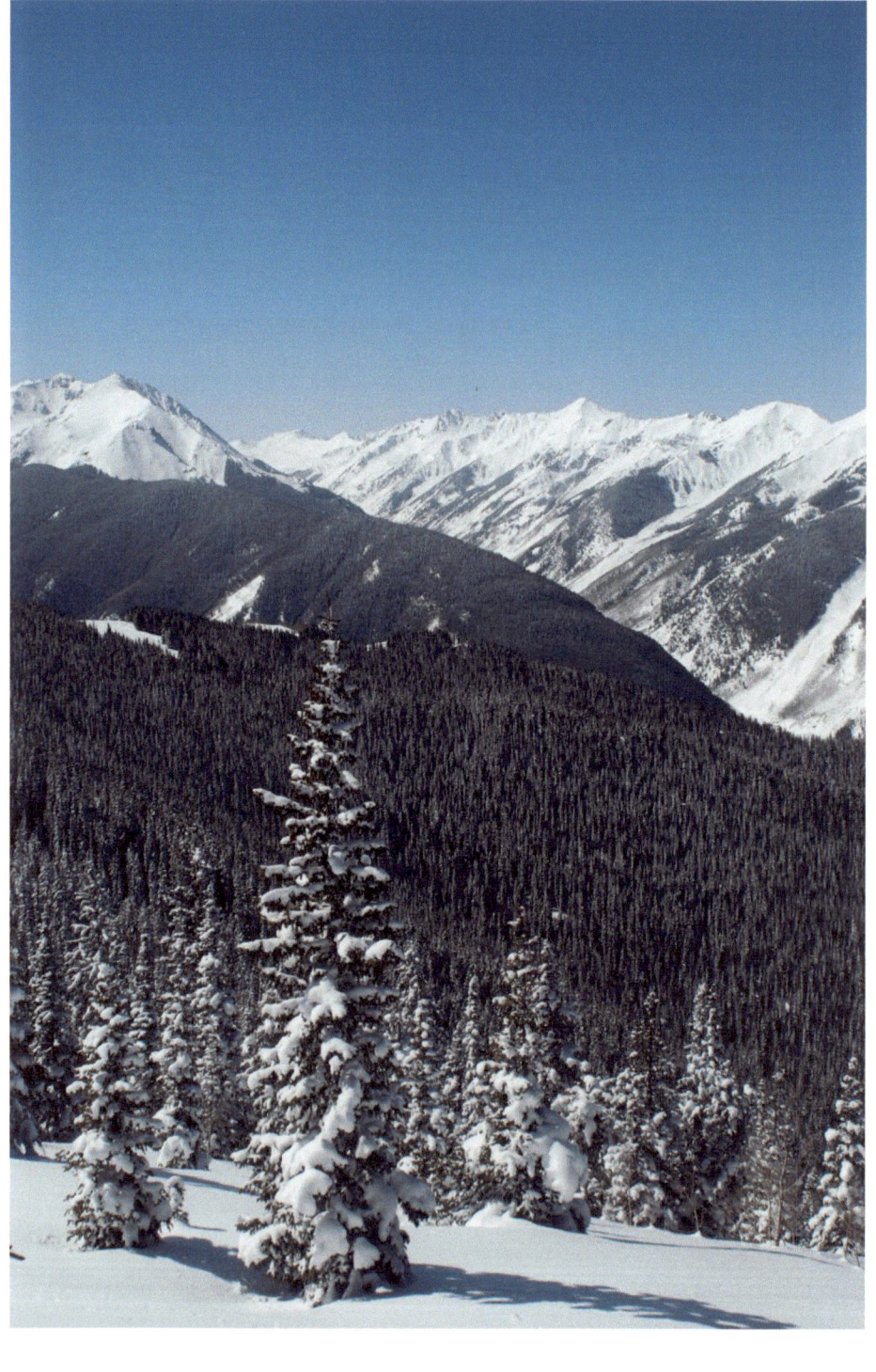

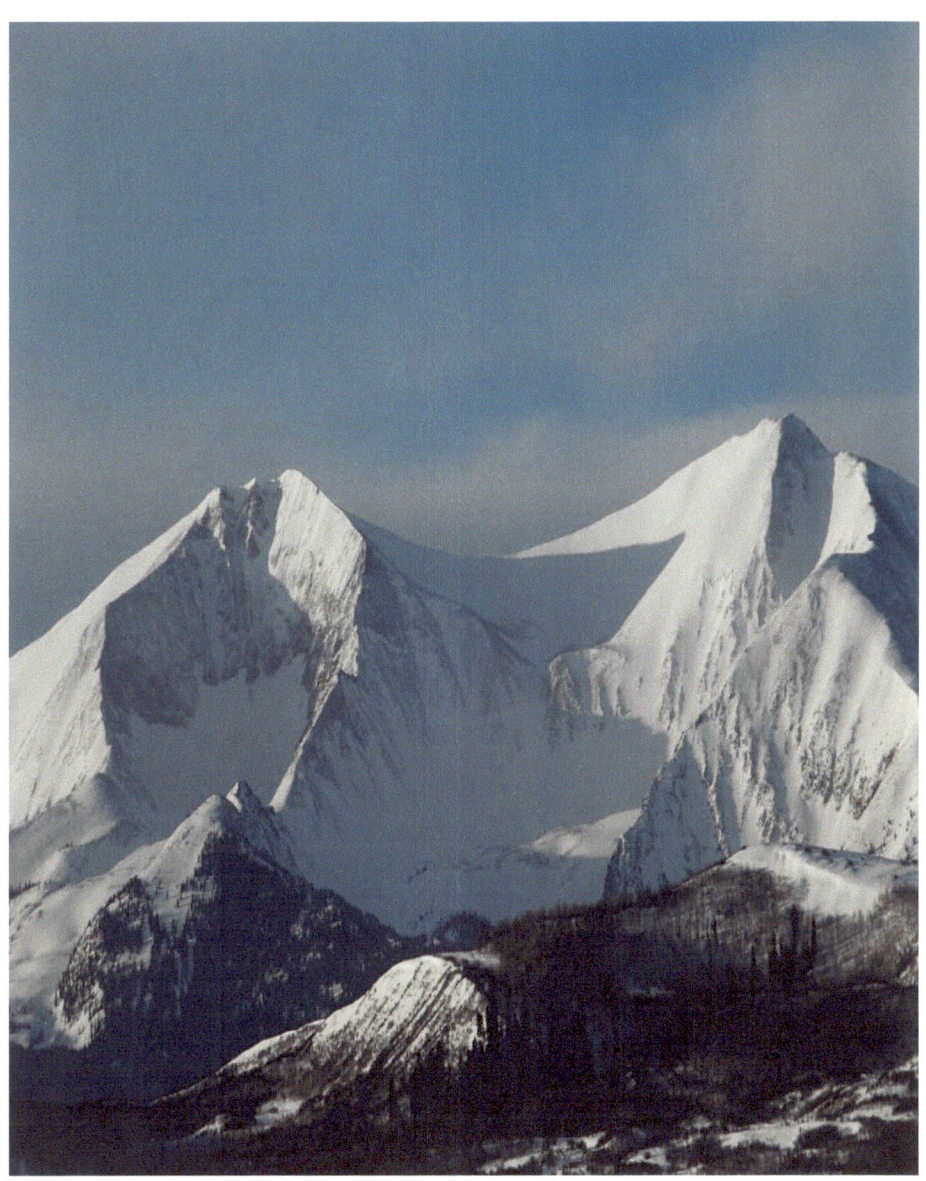

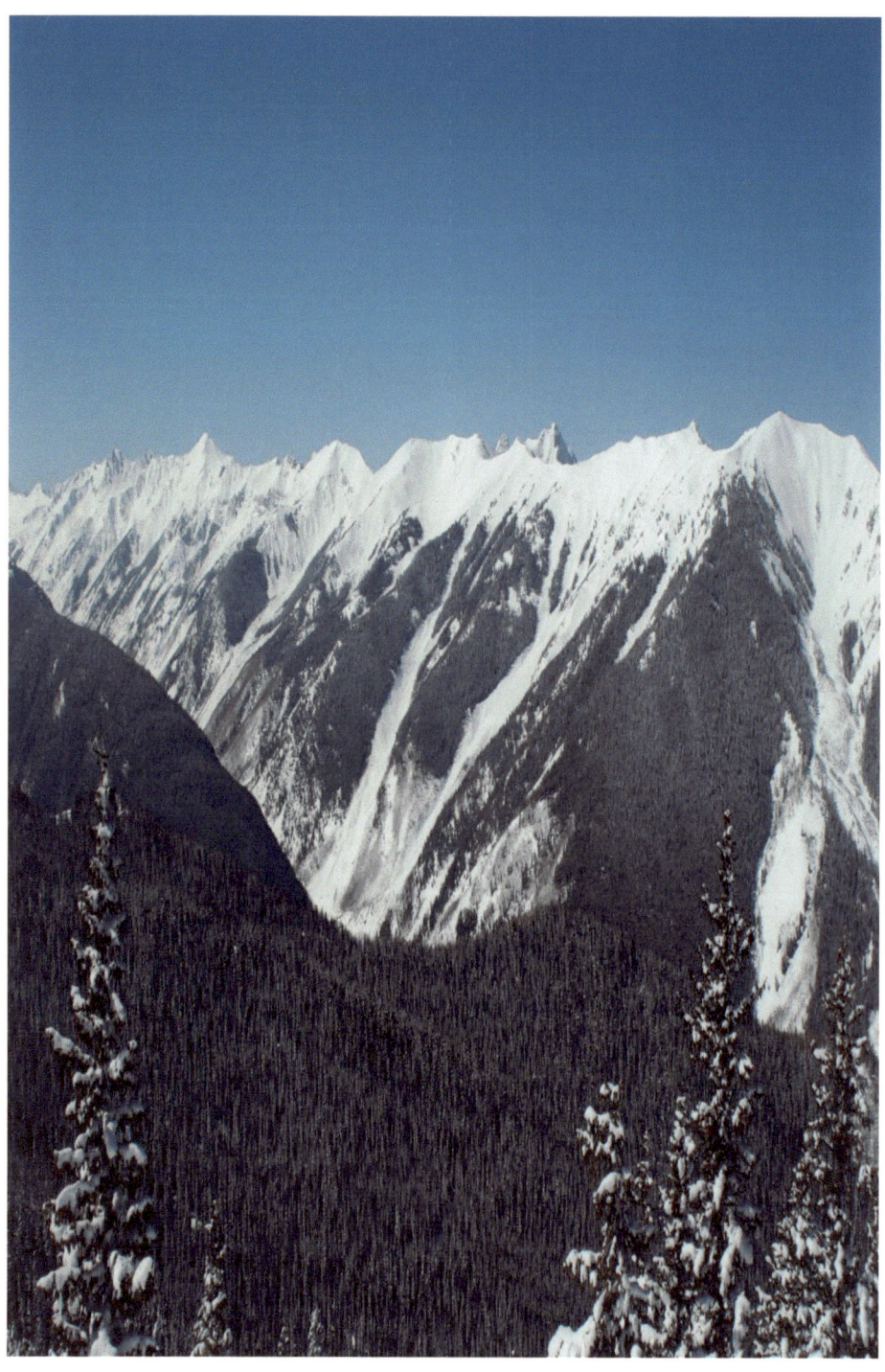

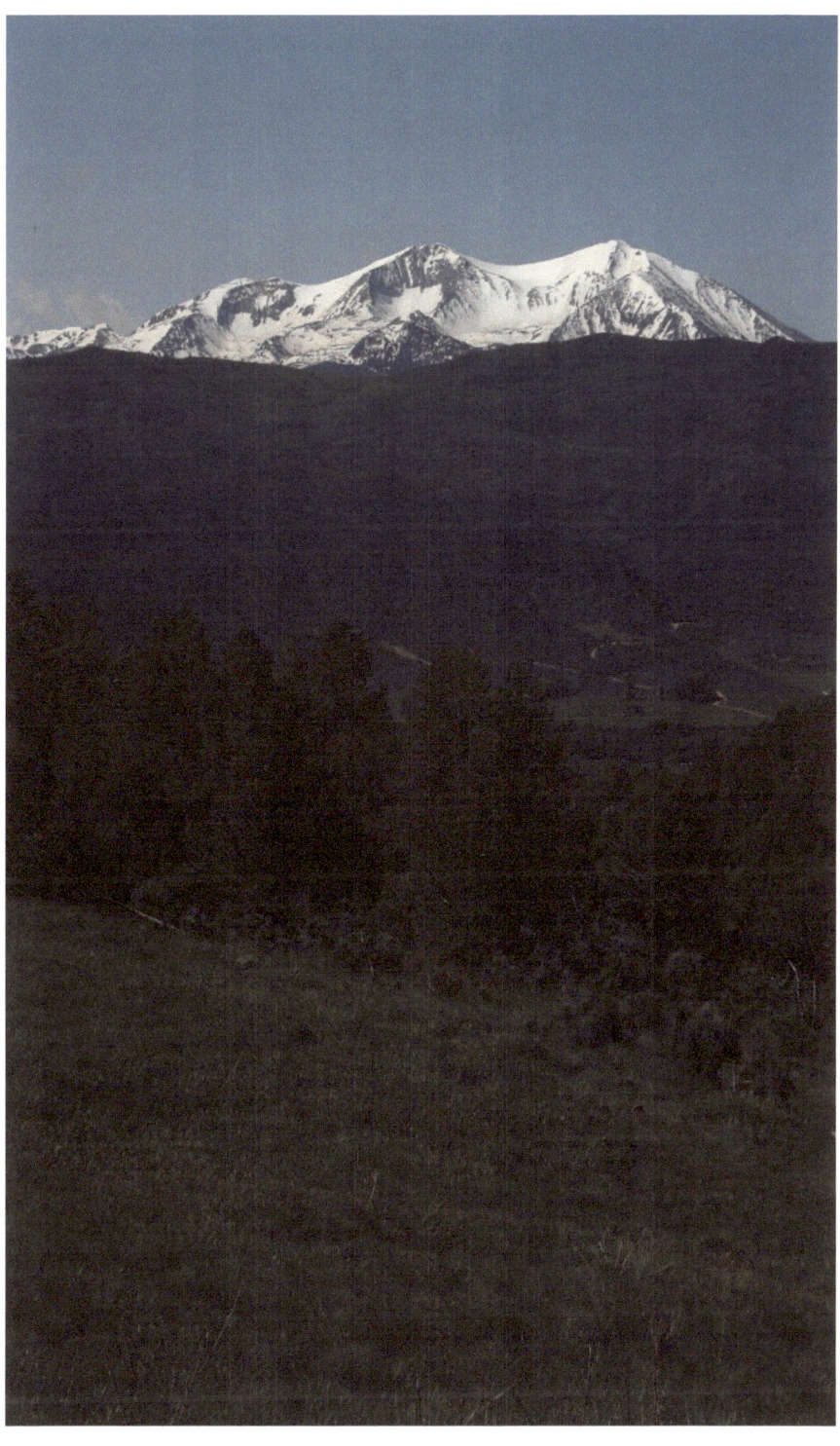

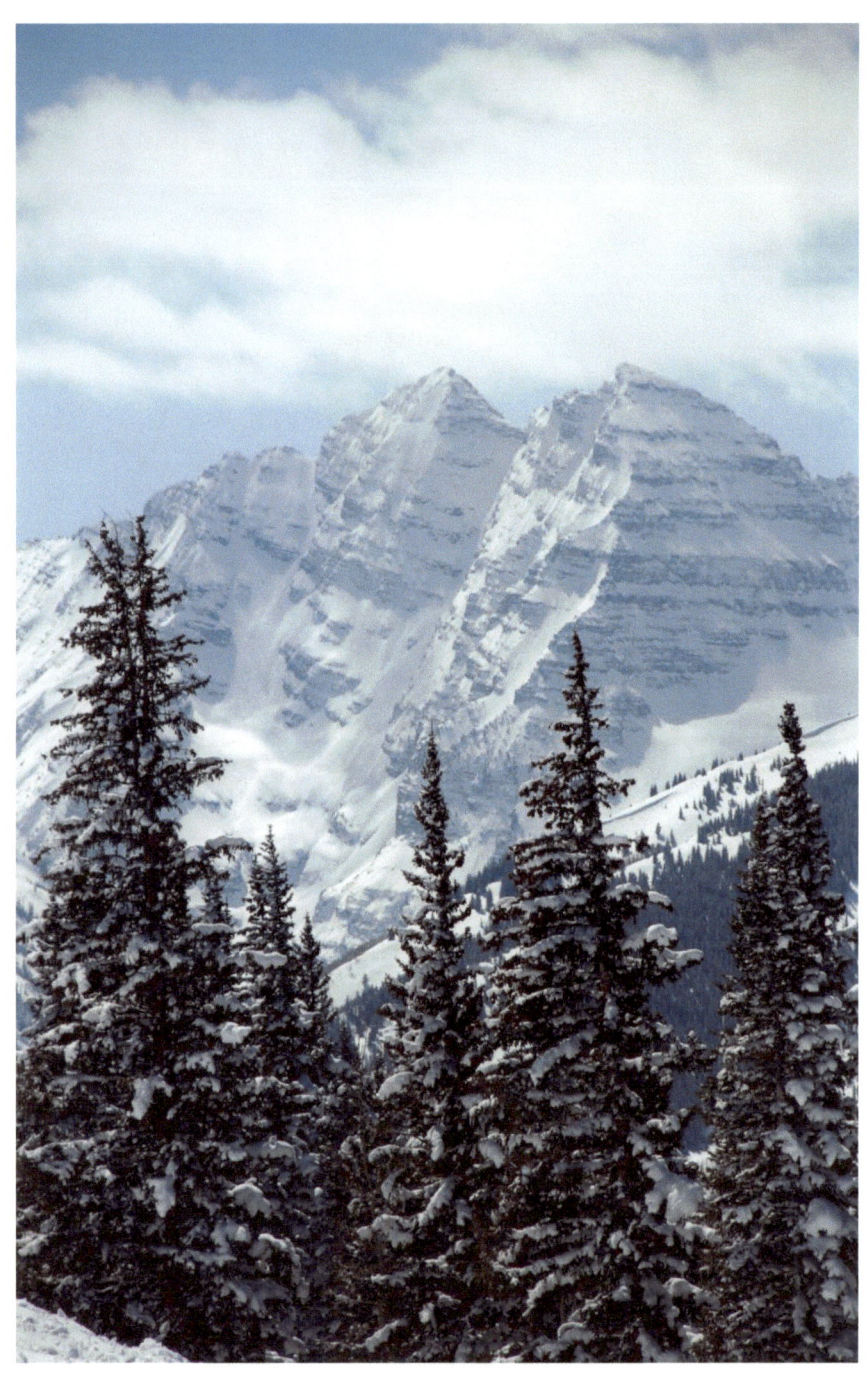

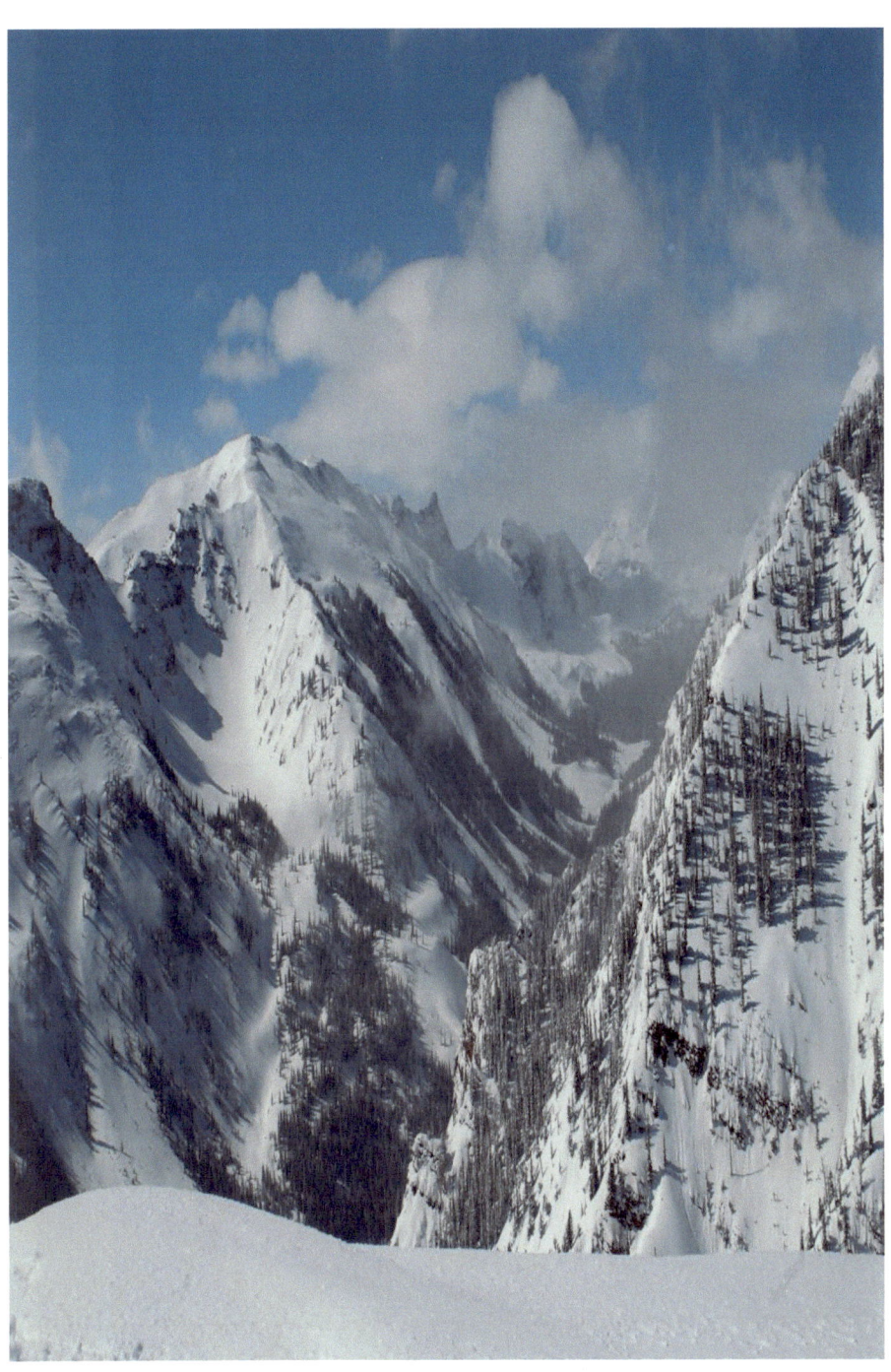

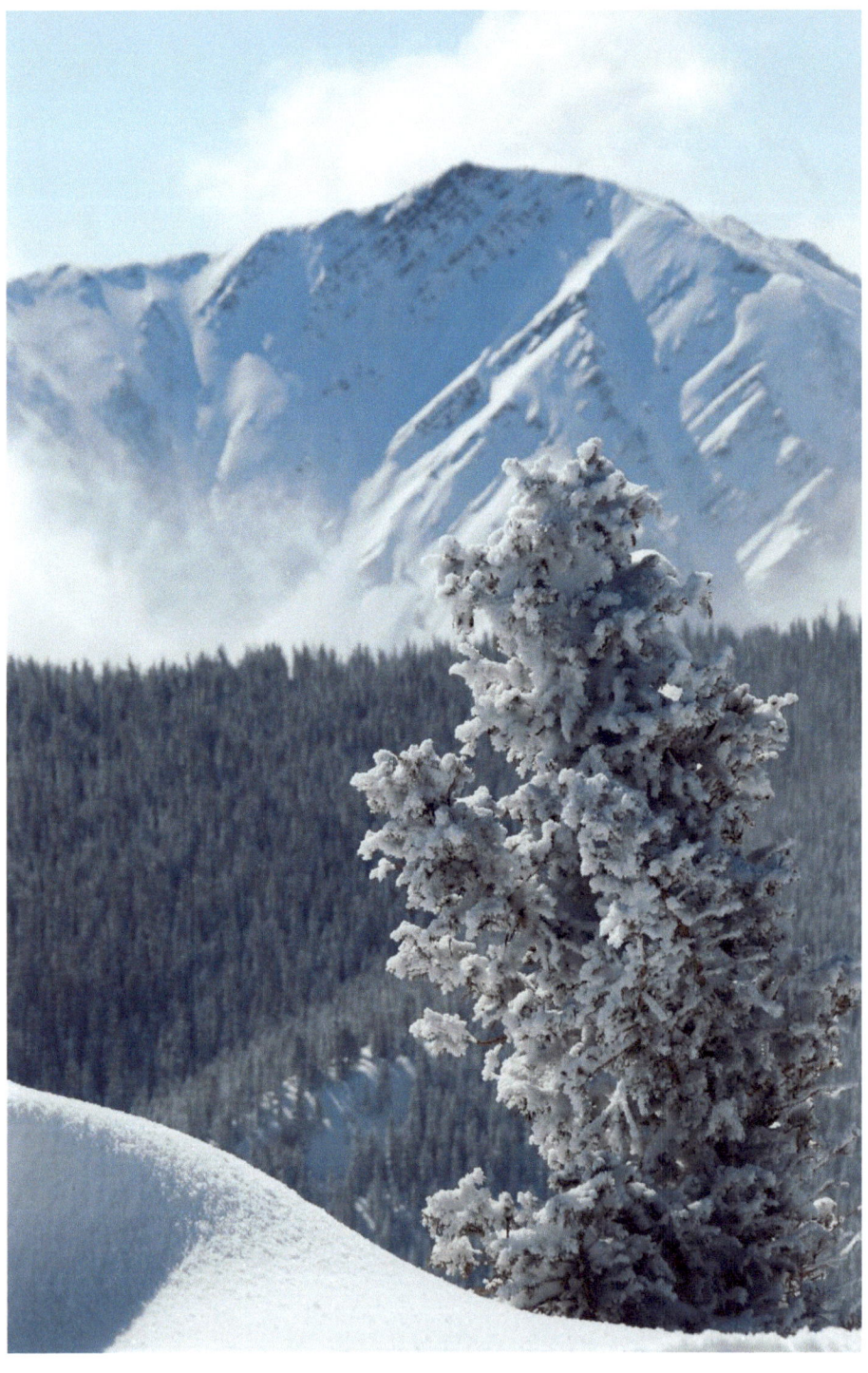

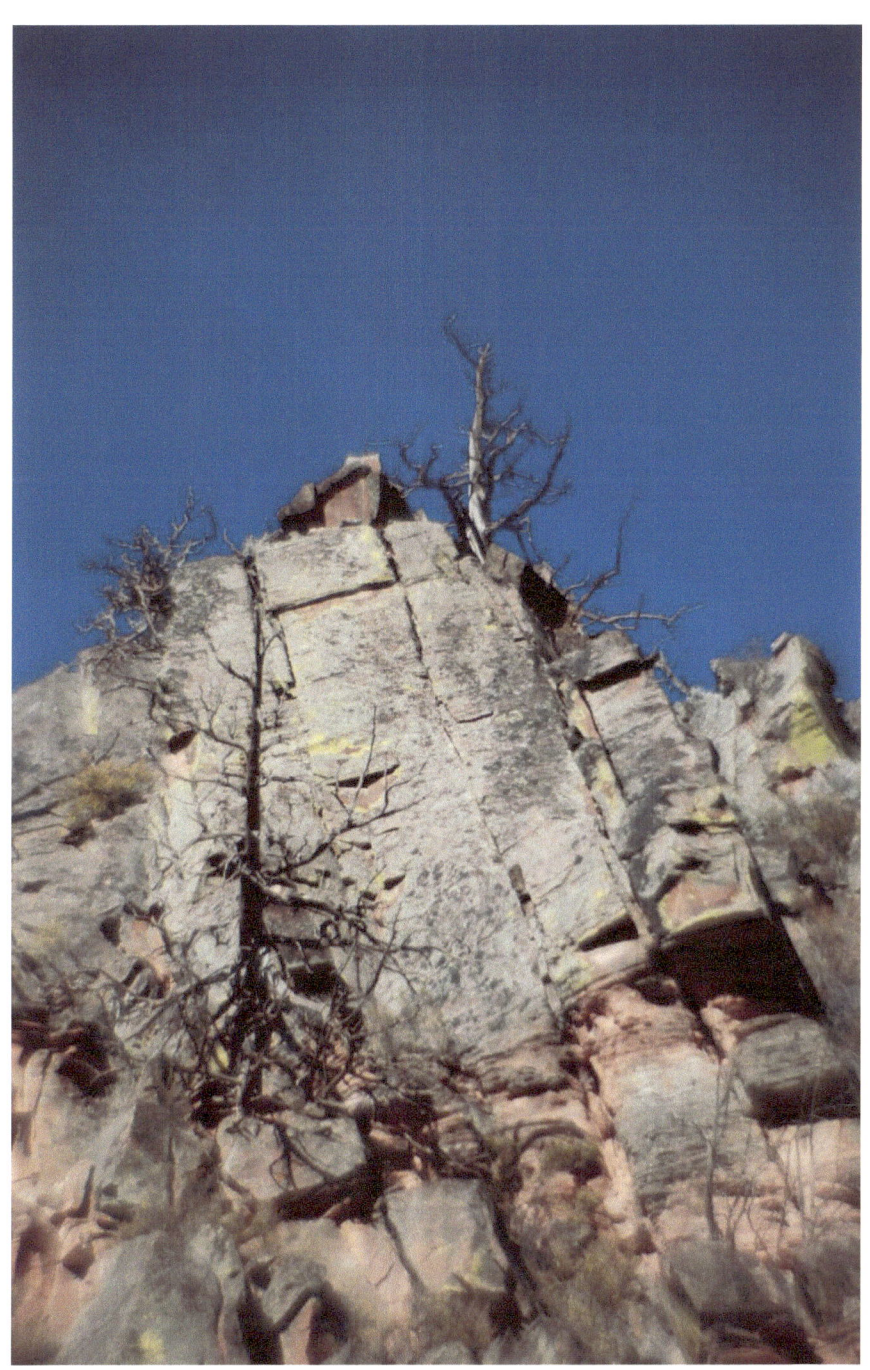

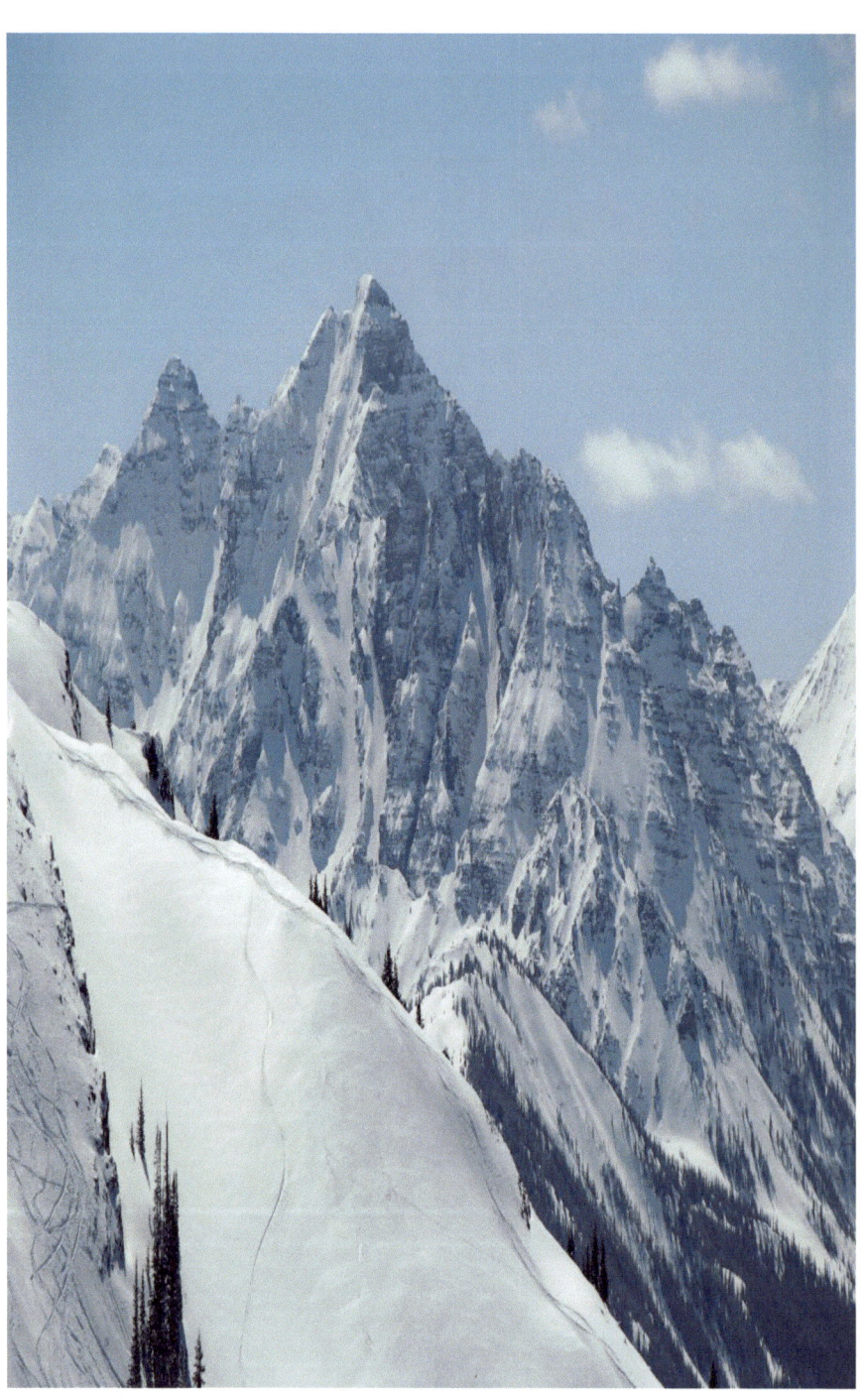

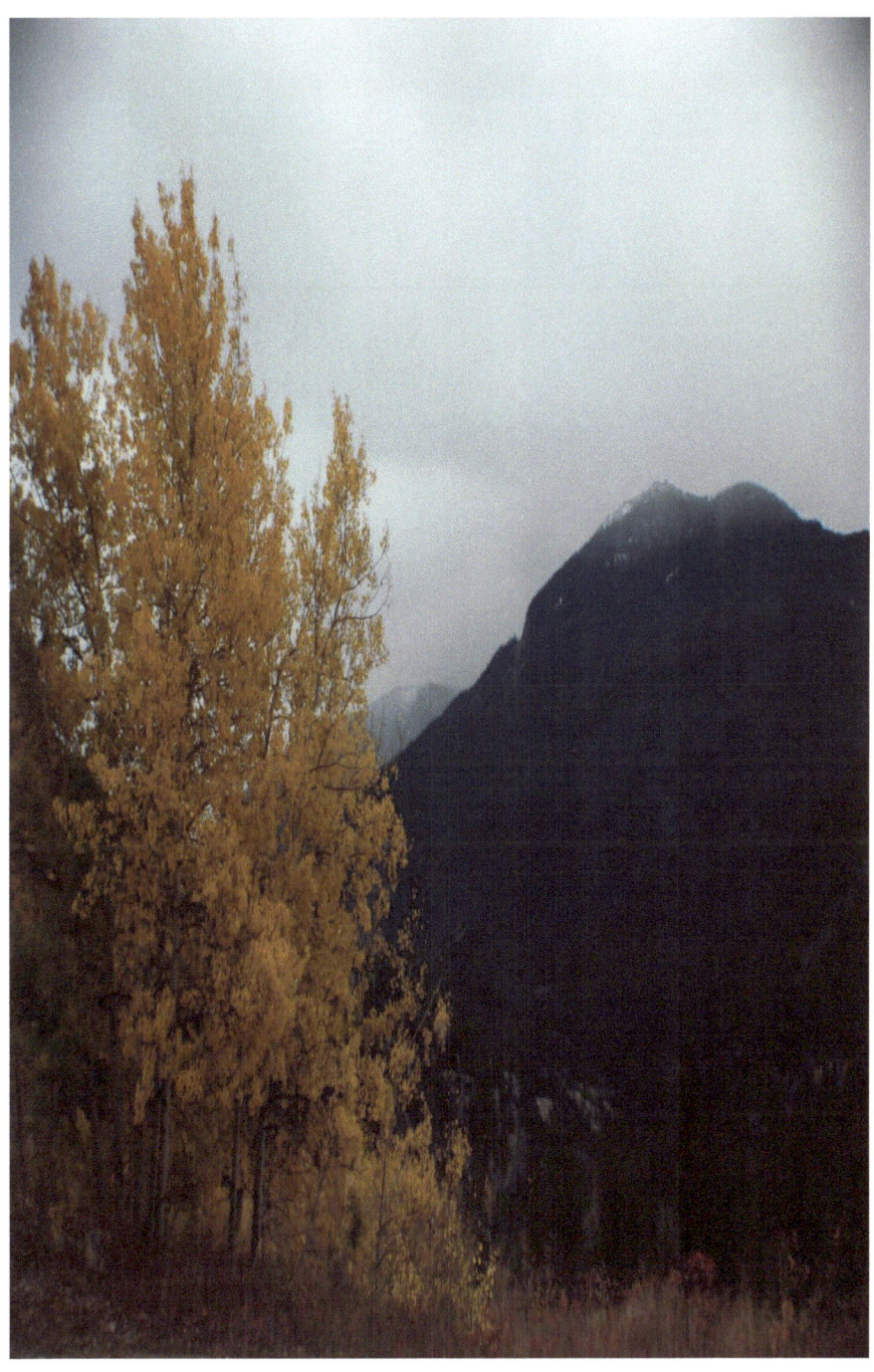

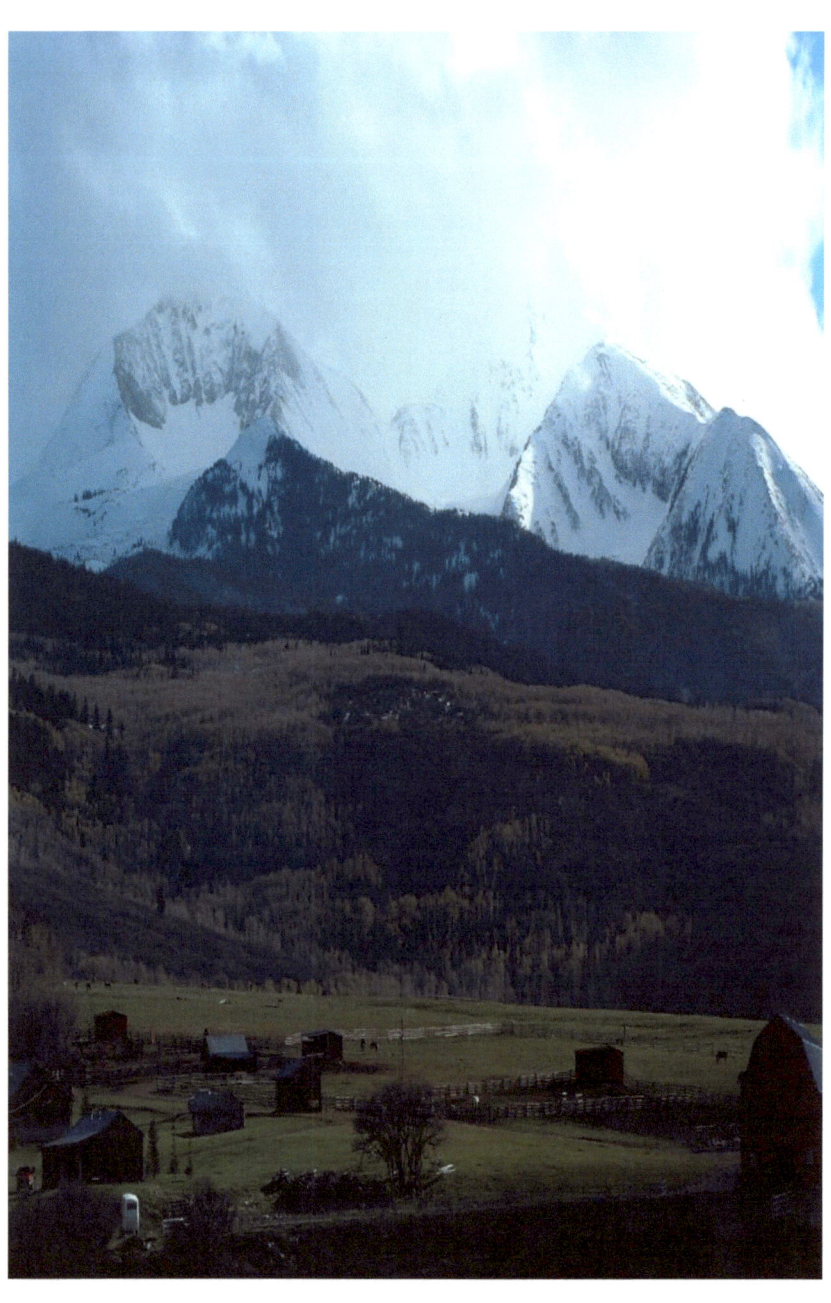

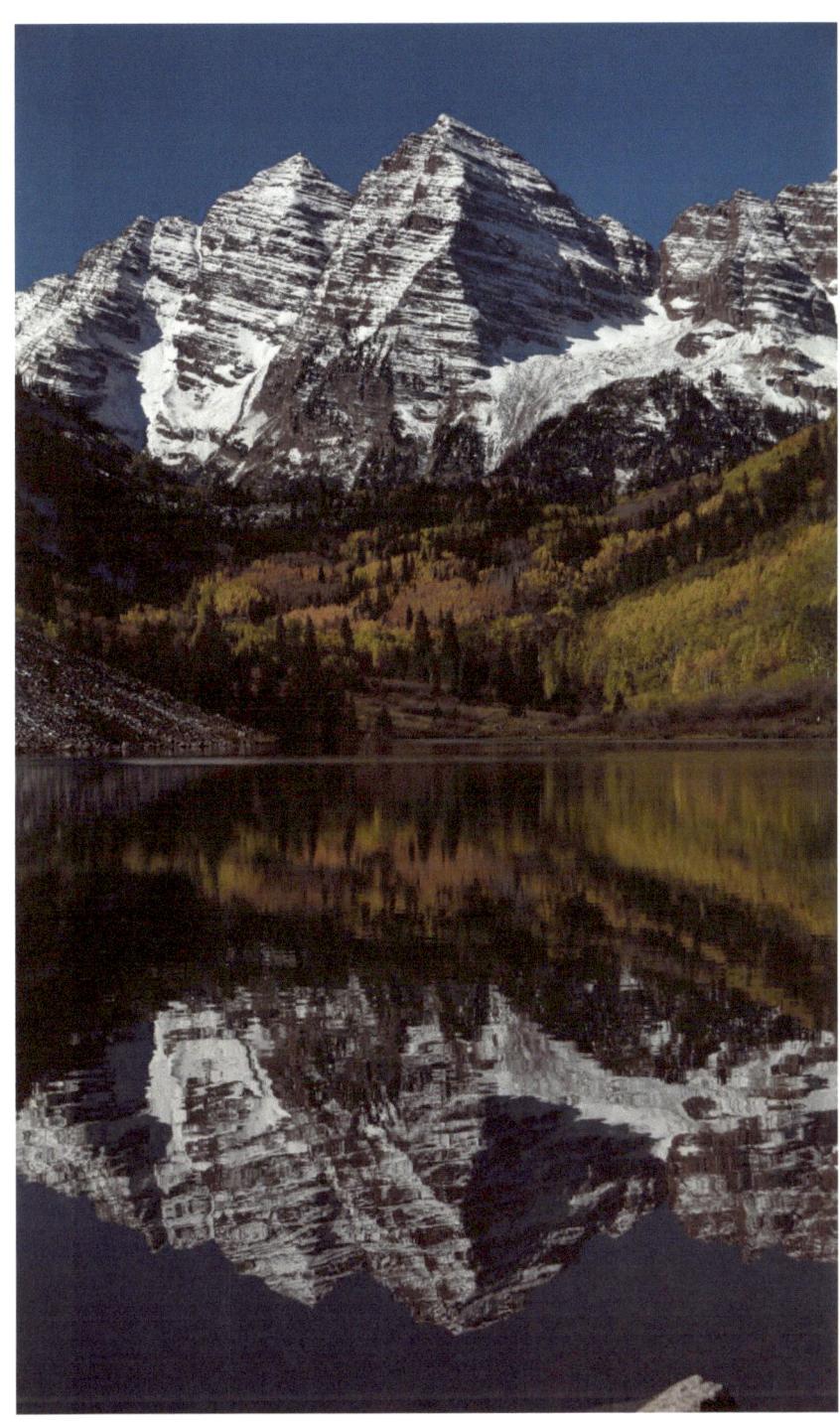

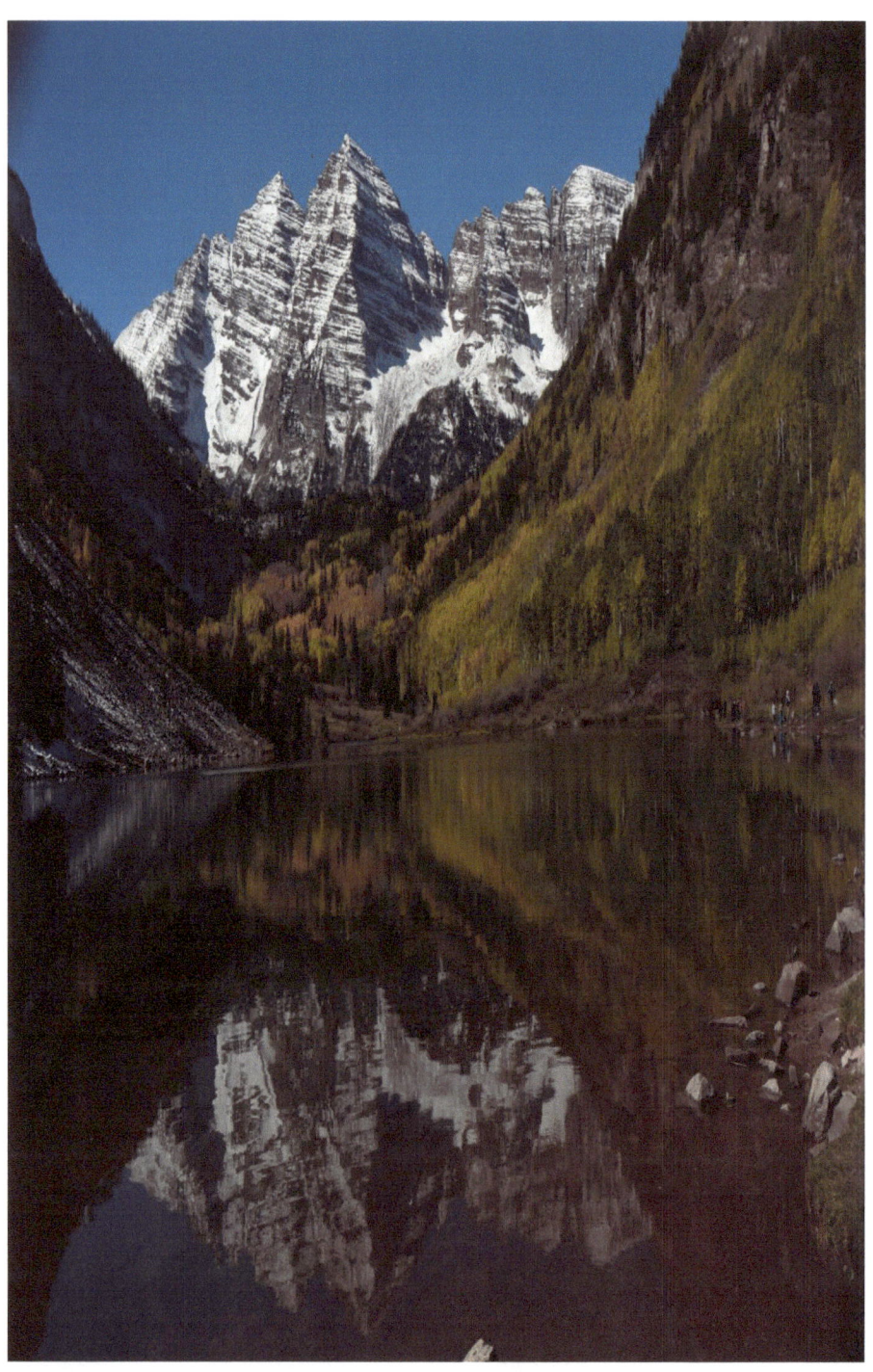

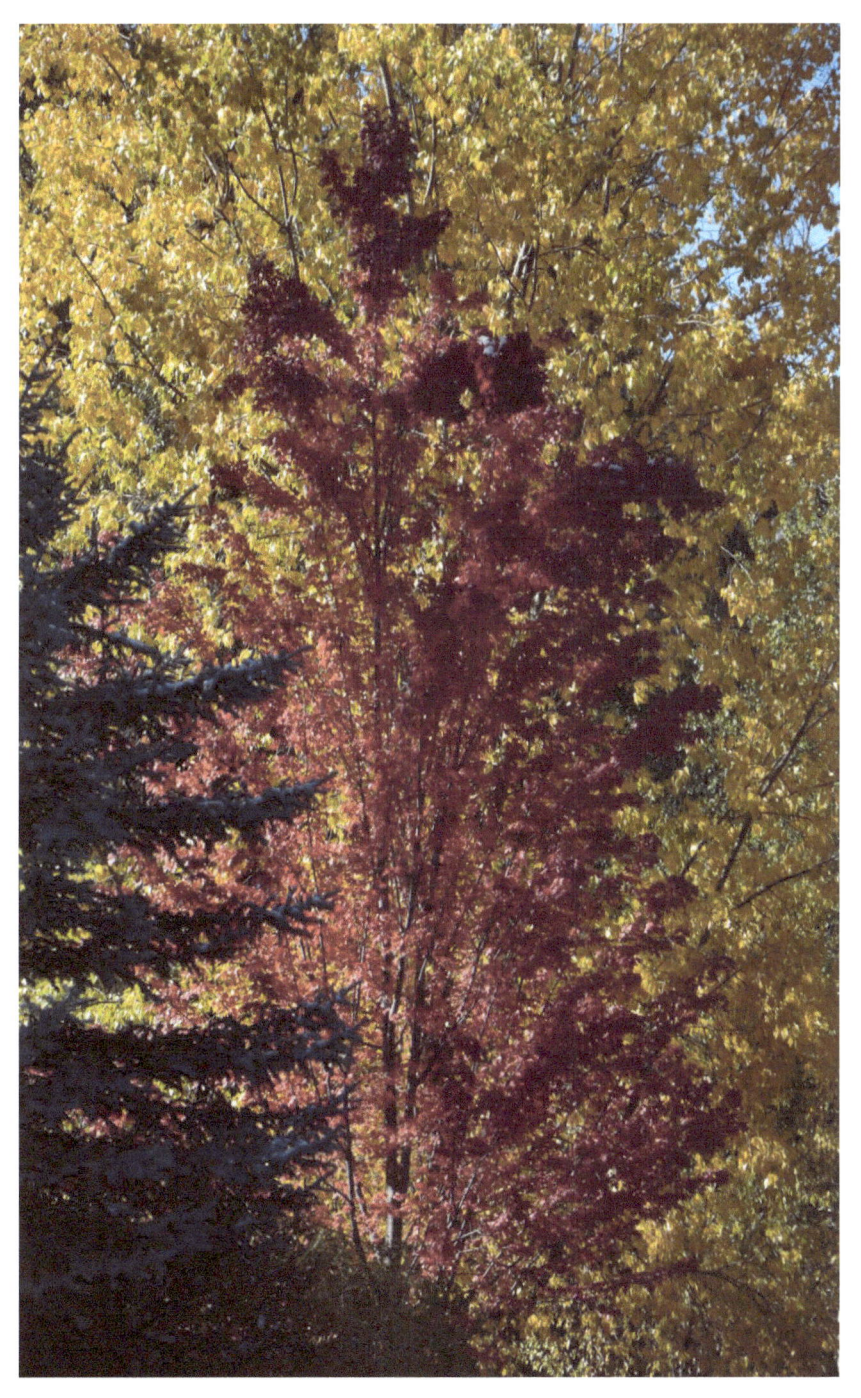

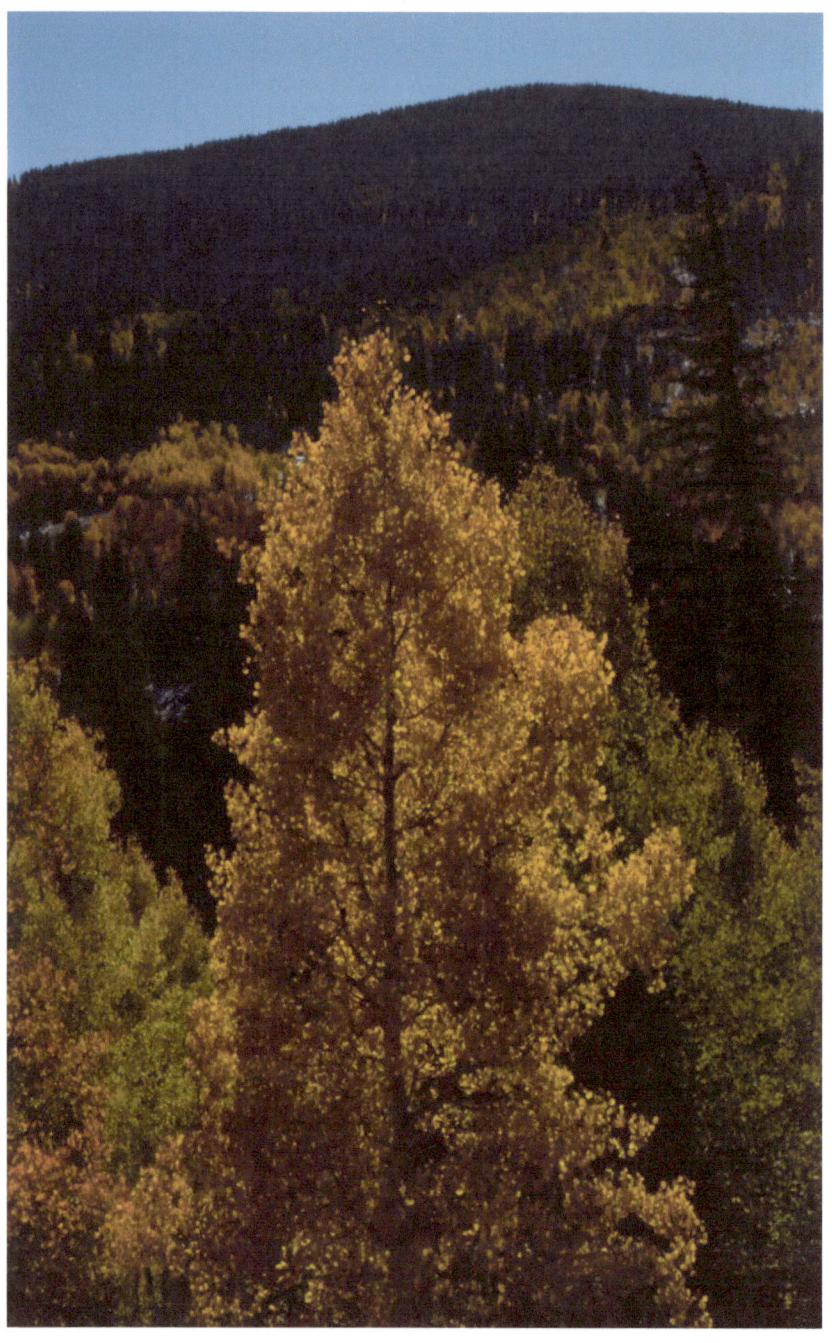

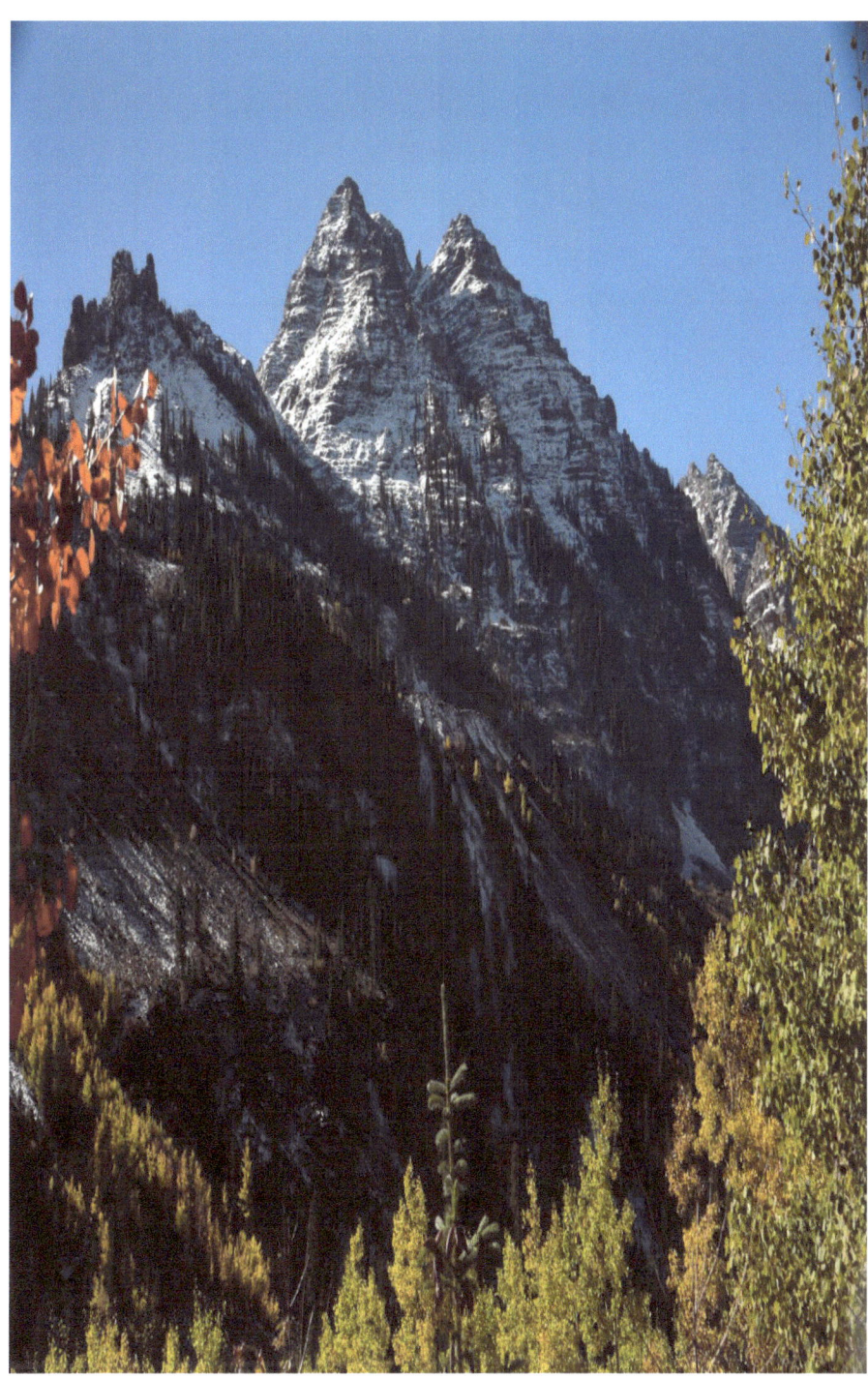

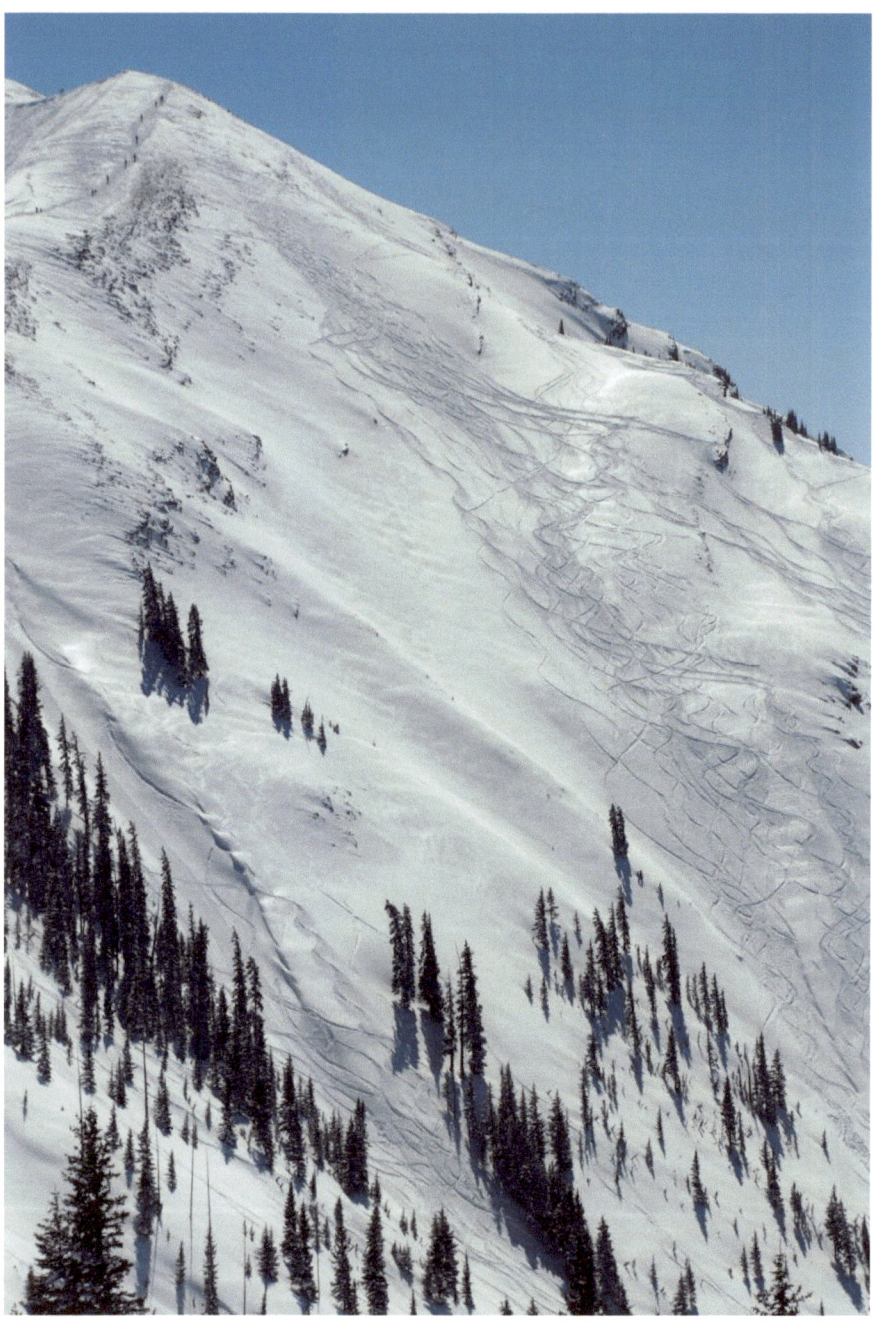

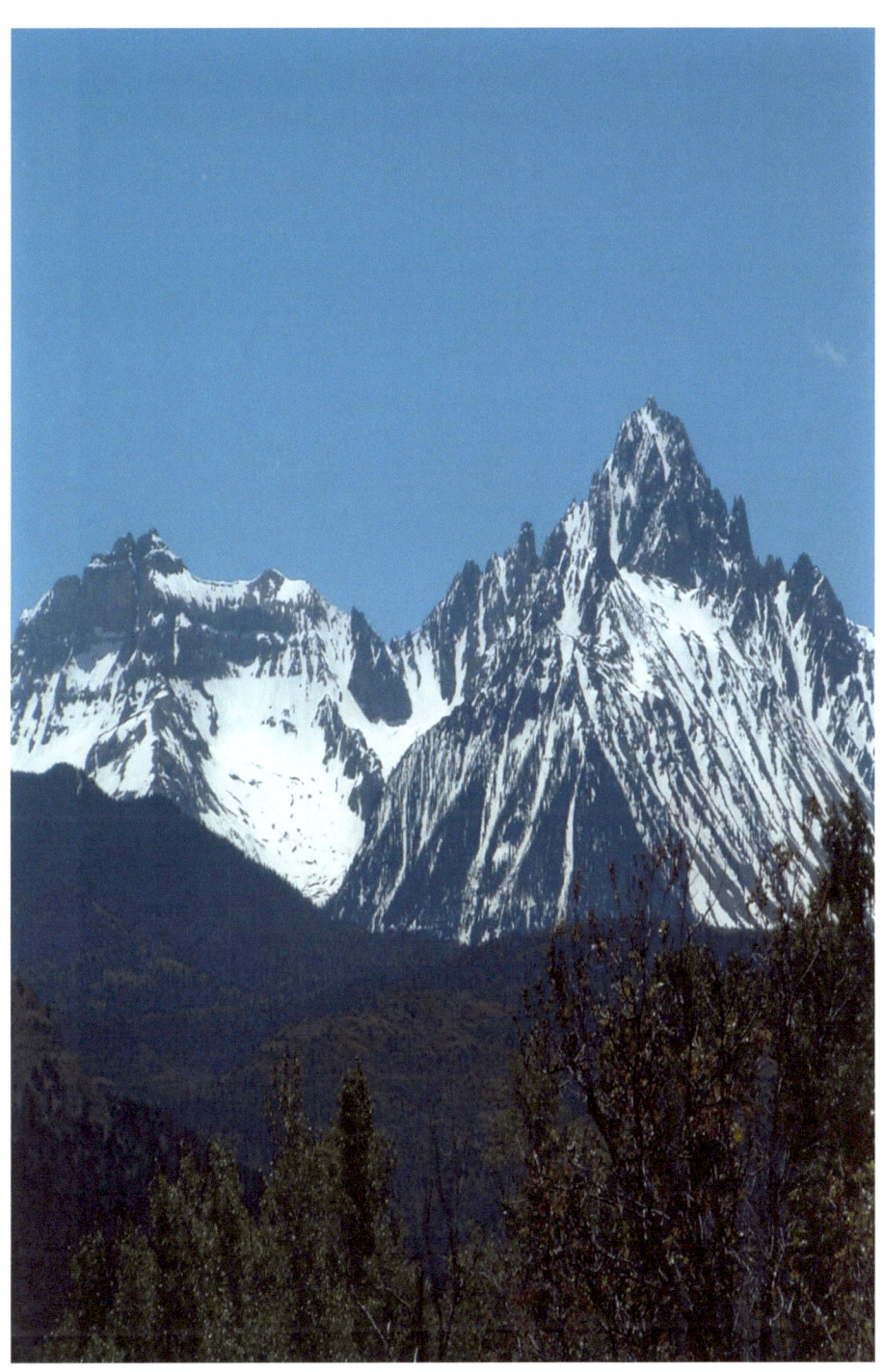

www.ingramcontent.com/pod-product-compliance
Lightning Source LLC
Chambersburg PA
CBHW041613180526
45159CB00002BC/841